★ AMERICA'S ★
Quilted Garden Blocks
Faye Labanaris

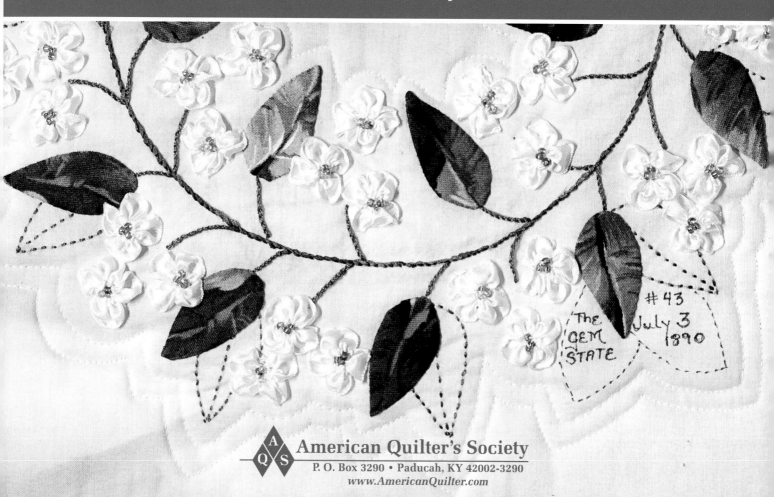

THE
GEM
STATE

#43

July 3
1890

American Quilter's Society

P. O. Box 3290 • Paducah, KY 42002-3290

www.AmericanQuilter.com

Located in Paducah, Kentucky, the American Quilter's Society (AQS) is dedicated to promoting the accomplishments of today's quilters. Through its publications and events, AQS strives to honor today's quiltmakers and their work and to inspire future creativity and innovation in quiltmaking.

EXECUTIVE BOOK EDITOR: ANDI MILAM REYNOLDS
COPY EDITOR: CHRYSTAL ABHALTER
GRAPHIC DESIGN: ELAINE WILSON
COVER DESIGN: MICHAEL BUCKINGHAM
PHOTOGRAPHY: CHARLES R. LYNCH

Additional copies of this book may be ordered from the American Quilter's Society, PO Box 3290, Paducah, KY 42002-3290, or online at www.AmericanQuilter.com.

Text © 2011, Author, Faye Labanaris
Artwork © 2011, American Quilter's Society

Library of Congress Cataloging-in-Publication Data

Labanaris, Faye.
  America's quilted garden blocks / by Faye Labanaris.
    p. cm.
  Includes bibliographical references.
  ISBN 978-1-60460-007-0
  1. Appliqué–Patterns. 2. Quilting–Patterns. 3. Album quilts.
4. State flowers in art. I. Title.
  TT779.L228 2011
  746.44'5–dc23
                      2011025396

COVER: Nine different state block details. Full quilts begin on page 15.

TITLE PAGE: IDAHO, quilt instructions on page 29

Dedication

To the natural beauty, diversity, and enduring spirit of America, and to flower lovers and quilters the world over.

Enjoy!

ABOVE: IOWA, quilt instructions on page 33

Acknowledgments

A person can make a quilt by themselves, but writing a book is a different story. It takes many people to ensure its arrival in the hands of the reader. As a seasoned author, I am still realizing just how much of a group effort it is to produce a book. To all those involved in the many stages of this book's production at AQS, I thank you very much for such a wonderful job!

Thank you to:

American Quilter's Society's president, Meredith Schroeder, for many years of publishing my ideas into beautiful books and your support throughout. It has been a pleasure to work with such a fine, professional, and personable company. Thank you for your extra attention to this project.

Executive book editor, Andi Reynolds, an editor's editor and most importantly, my editor. Your support, encouragement, excitement, and gentle guidance for this project have been very important and heartwarming to me.

The AQS design team, especially to Michael and Elaine, for a job more than well done!

Heather and Bob Purcell, for Superior Threads
Darlene Christopherson, for Hobbs Tuscany Collection Silk and
    Wool battings
Ellen Peters, for beautiful machine quilting
Pam Holland, for sharing her Drappliqué technique
Eugenia Barnes and Vivien Sayre, AQS certified quilt appraisers, for
    appraising the quilts
Pamela Byers, for being a good friend and project cheerleader
Joanna Samaras and Shirley Marino, for sewing on quilt labels on
    the 4th of July

My family for supporting me to do what makes me happiest outside of family, especially to my husband, Nick. Without his care of the family and technical computer skills, my books would not have been possible!

Faye Labanaris

Preface

I have always loved flowers. When I began teaching appliqué on a professional level in the early 1990s, I offered the groups that hired me an original wreath design of the state flower of the event or class I was leading. Over the years I had designed about a dozen wreaths. I knew that one day I would like to design a wreath for each of the United States. I sent this concept to AQS and my book proposal was accepted. Then I began the fun journey of creating designs for the remaining states' flowers. I actually felt sad when the last wreath was completed. It was a challenging project and a true labor of love. I hope you enjoy using this book as much as I did creating it, and have fun learning about our different state flowers and other fun facts. God bless America.

ABOVE: DELAWARE, quilt instructions on page 24

RIGHT: HAWAII, quilt instructions on page 27

Contents

On the CD*

Note: Use the zoom feature on your computer to see every detail of each block/quilt.

PUERTO RICO, quilt instructions on CD page 120

* If you do not have computer printing access, take the CD to your library or an office store, or call AQS for alternate pattern arrangements.

Basic Tips & Techniques

The sewing instructions for each state flower refer to this chapter, so be sure to read it before starting your project.

These state flower blocks call for hand appliqué, traditional piecing, silk ribbon embroidery, and wire-edged ribbon work, plus a little fabric painting and inking. Feel free to use your favorite techniques for these methods.

Silk ribbon embroidery uses narrow ribbon that is threaded through a needle eye to sew or embroider petals, leaves, etc., onto fabric. Other ribbon work involves manipulating wire-edged ribbon. There are a few basic supplies to have on hand and rules and sewing tips to follow when working with either.

Supplies

☆ Beads

Assorted sizes and colors create or embellish flower centers, especially the yellows and golden browns.

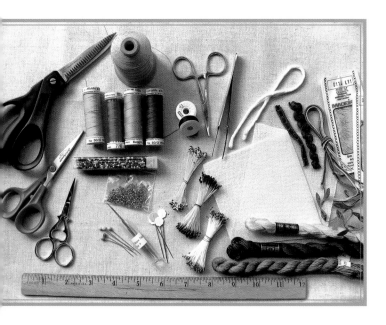

☆ Crinoline

Use this lightweight stabilizer for layering flowers. If you can't find crinoline, use an interfacing with some body that you can needle through.

☆ Embroidery floss

Shades of yellow and golden brown are best for flower centers. Embroider stamens to add a realistic look to your creations.

☆ Hair clips

Short and long varieties act as extra fingers to hold your work.

☆ Hemostats, pliers, or tweezers

These gripping tools allow you to hold on to the wire in wire-edged ribbon.

☆ Needles

Use milliner's needles sizes 9 and 10. These are long and sharp and perfect for working with ribbon. They can be used as beading needles, too. For hand appliqué, I like Roxanne™ appliqué needles—just one size, and it works for everyone.

☆ Pins

Use long, thin, flower-head pins or long silk pins.

☆ Ribbon

Available in sizes #3 (¾"), #5 (1"), #9 (1½"), wire-edged, unwired satin, Hanah Bias silk, velvet, jacquard, and picot-edge ribbons are just a few wonderful ribbons to work with.

The advantage to using wire-edged ribbon is that you can sculpt or mold flower petals into shapes and bend them forward or backward for realism. They are then sewn onto your fabric with hidden stitches.

With unwired ribbon, such as satin, the petals formed are uncontrollable, yet lovely. They are ruffled and more dimensional. You can control the ruffles with unwired ribbon by using anchoring stitches to hold the petals in place. I prefer working with Superior Threads silk ribbon for ribbon embroidery.

☆ **Ruler**

Have on hand a 12" ruler or a tape measure.

☆ **Scissors**

- ★ Inexpensive for cutting wire-edged ribbon, as the wire dulls the blades
- ★ Fabric scissors with a 4"–6" blade
- ★ Embroidery scissors with sharp, cut-to-the point tips

☆ **Thread**

Choose quilting thread or doubled regular sewing thread. A single strand of nylon beading thread can also be used. Do not use silk thread for stitching ribbon flowers; it is not strong enough. However, silk thread is perfect for hand appliqué. Use neutral thread for creating flowers, matching thread when attaching them to your project.

☆ **Trims**

Choose greens and browns for leaves and stems.

Working with Wire-edged Ribbon
Exposing the wire

To use the wire itself to gather the ribbon, simply hold the wire and gently slide the ribbon along the wired edge toward the middle section of the ribbon's length, gathering from both ends equally. Do not rush the process or pull too hard as the wire may break and you will have to resort to needle and thread to secure the ribbon. A gripping tool (see Supplies) is helpful in holding on to the wire.

Push down on the cut edge of the ribbon to expose a tiny bit of the wire on one side. Hold on to this wire with a gripping tool. Slide ½" to 1" of ribbon down the wire. Bend the wire over the ribbon to prevent the ribbon from sliding back onto the wire.

Repeat on the opposite end. Now you are ready to hold the wire and push the ribbon down to the center of the length for a gathered ribbon effect. Repeat on the other side. It is easier to gather into the middle rather than all the way down to the other end; there is less chance of wire breakage.

Dealing with broken wire

When gathering the ribbon on the wire, sometimes the wire breaks. This is not the end of your flower. Try and recover the wire end by poking it out through the edge of the ribbon and pushing the ribbon away from the wire so you will have enough wire to wrap around a bit of the ribbon to secure it. You may have to hand stitch the remaining unwired portion of ribbon.

How to handle a frayed selvage edge

This occurs when you pull the wire away from the ribbon at an angle. The wire is razor sharp and cuts right through the ribbon, resulting in a frayed edge. Immediately stop and secure the ribbon fray by wrapping the wire around the portion connected to the unexposed wired edge. To prevent this from happening, hold the ribbon and wire parallel to each other and slide the ribbon straight on down the wire.

Flowers

When sewing wire-edged ribbon into flowers, use a double strand of strong thread such as quilting thread, because much of the flower's construction involves gathering and pulling. Or, you may use a single strand of nylon beading thread.

Be sure to pull the gathers every few inches. This gather-as-you-sew process will prevent the thread from twisting and breaking.

Working with crinoline

In ribbon work, the flower petal arrangement is sewn onto a crinoline base.

Crinoline is a lightweight, stiffened netting similar to starched cheesecloth. If you can't find crinoline in the bridal department of a fabric shop, use a lightweight interfacing that has some body and can be needled through, or use a few layers of netting. Buckram is too heavy.

The flower is completely formed and tacked down with many stitches. The stitches are hidden through the many folds of ribbon. You can arrange the flower petals to your liking with these stitches.

When the flower is complete, the excess un-stitched crinoline is trimmed away from the flower. Do not make any stitches on the outer edge of the petals as these stitches may be cut away with the trimmed crinoline. The finished product is now ready to be attached to a quilt or garment with a few stitch-es of matching thread through the crinoline base.

Stitching wire-edged ribbon centers

Start with a tiny knot and then anchor this knot in place with a backstitch or two. Test with a gentle tug. Your knot should not slip through the ribbon. The stitch length should be a bit longer than when you are stitching fabric. The longer the stitch, the more pleats result and the smaller the opening of gathered ribbon centers. Smaller stitches result in more gathers in the ribbon and larger gathered ribbon centers.

Leaves

Flowers need leaves to complement them. Using a variety of green ribbons, fabrics, and trims will give richness to your floral creations. Wire-edged ribbon leaves can be stitched flattened for a subtle effect or left dimensional for a realistic effect. Fabric leaves can be appliquéd for a flat look or seamed and turned to make a dimensional fabric leaf.

☆ Cut your leaves from a variety of shades of green fabrics. Save your scraps for this purpose.

☆ Leaf veins can be drawn on the fabric with a permanent fabric pen.

☆ Leaf veins can be embroidered on the fabric with contrasting thread(s) by hand or machine.

☆ Cut a wholecloth leaf from a printed fabric leaf. Select it with a window template.

☆ An Ultrasuede® leaf is cut exactly to its final shape. The outer edges can be further cut with fine serrations for a serrated- or tooth-edged leaf.

☆ Ribbon leaves from variegated ribbon can be appliquéd as fabric leaves.

☆ A split leaf adds interest with a combination of fabric colors, prints, and textures. Fabric sugges-tions: corduroy, velvet, ribbon.

☆ Decorative green trim can be folded into a leaf shape for a textural variation. This leaf is formed on crinoline and attached where desired on the block.

☆ Appliquéd fabric leaves can be enhanced with an embroidery stitch added around the outer edge. The stitch can be an outline, stem, or chain stitch. The thread used can be matching or contrasting, de-pending on the look you want to achieve.

☆ Seam and turn fabric leaves for a dimensional fold-over effect with a contrasting back fabric.

Stems

There are so many beautiful kinds of flowers to make, why limit yourself to using just one type of stem? There is no end in sight once you start think-ing of stems whenever you see anything greenish or brownish.

Although fabric is the traditional medium to use for stems, it can be fun to try a little variation. Add interest and texture to your stems with a variety of trims, cords, threads, and embroidery techniques. Just about any green or brown cording or trim will work. Once you start working with trims in your ap-pliqué, you'll seek out many sources for your collec-tion of supplies. If the yard or cord strand is too thin, just twist several lengths together for a twisted cord and couch it down into position.

Traditional bias stems

The traditional appliqué method involves cutting a strip of fabric on the bias between ¾" to 1" wide. Fold the strip in half through the width of the ribbon and place the two raw edges on the outer curve line of the drawn stem. Stitch a running stitch with small stitches about one quarter of the way down from the cut raw edges. Fold the strip over the cut edges and stitch down through the folded edge.

Here's a shortcut for cutting bias strips: A strip of ¾" or 1" wide masking tape placed on the bias of a piece of fabric makes a quick and easy cutting guide. Use fabric scissors.

Another method for making bias stems is to fold a 1" bias strip of fabric into thirds (through the width) and baste down the middle on the machine. This method works great if you need a small amount of prepared bias stems.

You can also make prestitched bias stems with bias bars. Follow the directions on the packaging for stitching a variety of sizes of bias stems. These allow you to freely place bias stems on your design; however, both sides of the fabric must be sewn in place.

Fused bias stems

A quick method for bias stems is to use the fusible bias strips commercially available. These come on a roll in several shades of brown, green, black, and other colors. The bias strips can be placed in position and ironed down on the fabric. Stitch down afterwards for permanent placement. The disadvantage to this method is that you are limited in the colors that you can use.

Here's a trick for really skinny stems: Fold the fusiable bias stems in half through the width and iron with the fusible sides together for ⅛" stems. Couch down to create those tiny stems that connect to the main stem.

Embroidered stems

Stems can also be embroidered by hand or machine. If making by hand, a stem, outline, or chain stitch works well. There are many wonderful threads available for embroidery. Don't hesitate to combine threads for a new look. Use one thread or more depending on the effect you want. If you can thread it through the eye of a needle, then you should be able to embroider with it. If embroidering by machine, a narrow satin stitch would work nicely for a stem.

Twisted ribbons

Narrow #3 (¾") wire-edged ribbon can be tightly twisted to form a stem. It can be bent into any shape and couched down into place on your background fabric. It can also make a lovely stem for a flower corsage or arrangement on a covered box.

Couched stems

If a thread you wish to use for a stem is too thick for the eye of the needle, then consider couching it in place. Couching involves laying down thread, yarn, or cord on the drawn stem line and anchoring it in position with a thinner thread in a matching or contrasting color sewn in small stitches across the thicker thread.

An easy way to couch cording is to first draw the line of the stem's shape on the fabric (pencil works well). Then draw over this line with a toothpick dipped into glue. Place the cording carefully over the glued line and press gently to hold. Only glue a few inches at a time because it does dry quickly. After the glue dries you can couch the trim in place with matching or contrasting thread.

The advantage to couching is that you can use a narrow width of any type of trim for tiny stems or a textured trim for hairy or thorny stems. The texture adds interest to the block and makes "sewing" stems fast, fun, and easy.

Take care with selecting the stem's starting and ending points. Be sure they will be hidden under a leaf, bud, or flower.

Ultrasuede

Cut a narrow strip of Ultrasuede for a stem in any shape and width you want. The raw edge is stitched down and you are done.

Square U Technique for Round Petal Flowers

Square U Technique for Round Petal Flowers

There are several different stitching techniques for producing round flower petals. With traditional ruching, round petals are formed on both sides of the stitching line. With the square U technique, the petals are formed on only one side of the stitching line.

The advantage to this method is that the petals can be made individually from small pieces of ribbon or all together from longer lengths of ribbon to form a chain of petals. The petals are then stitched onto a crinoline base and the center opening is filled with a padded center, beads, knotted trim, or your choice of materials.

The size of the petals will vary with the width of the ribbon used and the measured stitching distance between the ends of the square U. Both wire-edged and unwired ribbon can be used. Don't be afraid to experiment for variation in your petals.

Stitching round-petaled blossoms

Using #3 ribbon (¾"), allow 1" for each petal plus an additional ½" at either end for the tails.

Always remove the wire from the bottom edge. This is the bottom of the U and becomes the center of the flower. If you leave the wire in, the stitched center opening will be too large and will also prove difficult in gathering the ribbon.

Follow the figure, pin the measured intervals on the ribbon. Begin stitching the square U pattern on the first petal: Stitch down, across the bottom, up, loop over the selvage, and stitch down the width of the ribbon to the first pin.

Give the thread a gentle pull to form the first petal.

Stitch across the bottom edge, then up, loop, then stitch down to the second pin and pull again to form the second petal. Repeat along the length of the ribbon. Form each petal separately to avoid tangles and broken thread.

When all the petals are formed, connect the first and last petals in a circle or spiral or cone. The color of the petals is the color of the unstitched ribbon area if using ombre ribbon.

Secure the petals onto a square of crinoline. Tuck the ribbon tails into the center opening to form a basis for the center details. If you do not have enough tail material to fill the center, then use scraps of ribbon to fill in this area. This provides a slightly raised area for center detail, such as beading.

Fill the center opening with your choice of details, such as beading, French knots, trim, etc.

Wire ribbon allows you to sculpt the petals so they can be arranged to become fuller or to be shaped as pointy tipped petals. Variations:
★ Increase the stitching distance to 1¼" on a 6" length of ribbon and a four-petal posy results.
★ Experiment using different widths for the stitching distance.

Lettering and Writing on Fabric

Inked banners and scrolls add wonderful focal points in which to place your signature, a date, and the name of the piece—on the front of your work. Be proud! And *don't be afraid*—go forth and ink with much pleasure and successful accomplishment.

Using a fabric pen or ink adds wonderful details to your project. Here are tips that will help you to ink beautifully and fearlessly on fabric.

Always pretest all marking pencils and pens on scraps of the fabrics you are planning to use. Although the marking tools are made to strict specifications, fabrics are not; they vary as to chemical dye and finish, which affect how inks and pencil react.

Pigma® Micron® pens are a good choice for fabric lettering. The ink is permanent and acid-free. Begin with a black pen size #01 and soon you'll want to go on to various colors and widths. There are many other markers available; just be sure to test them.

Draw or write what you want to put on your fabric piece first on paper for proper spacing and a general appearance test. You may trace or write your design or words on fabric using a mechanical lead .05 pencil. Write with a very light touch. First test the pencil to be sure it can be erased completely and cleanly from your fabric. Also, test your eraser to be sure it doesn't leave a smudge.

Iron freezer paper onto the back of your fabric after you have the pencil tracing completed. This stabilizes the fabric and turns it into a stiff surface for inking ease. You can also use wide masking tape on the back of your fabric to stabilize it.

Using a light touch, gently ink over the pencil lines. You may have to ink over the lines several times. You can always make it darker, but you can't make it lighter!

For each state flower block, use your best handwriting, either cursive or printing, for the state name. Use a ruler and write against the straight edge. If you are not sure about your handwriting, you can print out the state name from the large assortment of fonts available on your computer. Using a light box, trace it onto your background fabric.

For a calligraphic look, shade the letters in the words by thickening the down stroke.

Another choice is to use purchased stencils from an art supply or craft store. These letters can be enlarged or reduced on a copier to fit your space.

Your lettering can be embroidered to enhance the inking to add a nice bit of detail to your work.

Fabric Marker Appliqué

The term Drappliqué was coined by Pam Holland, quilt artist and teacher from Australia, for her technique of drawing with fabric markers for appliqué. I enjoyed learning this technique in a class, and with her permission, I have used it for several of the state flowers and present it in this book.

Drappliqué is perfect for those flowers that are just too delicate for any traditional method of appliqué or embroidery. It is also a lot of fun and brings back fond memories of childhood coloring. Feel free to use the technique for leaves, stems, buds, and lettering.

While there are lots of fabric markers available, the best seem to be Fabrico® by Tsukineko®. They have a wide range of colors and a dual tip (brush and point) in one pen.

I found that by just practicing a bit on scrap fabric, I was soon able to tackle the permanent placement of the flowers by drawing directly onto the background fabric with confidence.

It helps to have an outline of the flower with the individual petals marked out on the background fabric. This can be lightly drawn with a hard lead pencil.

To shade the petal, hold the pen at about the midway point and at an almost horizontal position. You are not holding it in a normal writing position. This gives you a loose grip so you won't be tempted to bear down and make too dark a stroke.

Your strokes should be light and feathery. You can always go back and make them darker, but you can't make them lighter.

Begin with the lightest shade first and leave white space at the flower's center and between the strokes.

Let dry, then shade with the next darker shade, using streaks. It will soon become apparent to you where to shade. Let dry between applications to prevent blending of the colors.

The last step is to outline the flower petals with a fine-point black marker to clearly delineate them.

Appliquéing with Ultrasuede

Using Ultrasuede is the easiest form of appliqué. Just cut the exact shape you desire, position the piece, and hand stitch the raw edges. It is a wonderful timesaver for tiny, delicate pieces such as bud cases, individual petals, berries, stems, and leaves.

Make a template of the pattern piece. Trace its reverse on the wrong (smooth) side of the Ultrasuede with a fine point marking pen.

Cut just barely outside the line with very sharp scissors. Position the piece and secure with a dot of glue. Stitch (secure) the outside edges with very fine thread. The closer together the stitches, the puffier the finished piece will be. *Optional: Embellish the sewn piece with outline embroidery.*

LEFT: MINNESOTA, full quilt shown on page 42.
Petals appliquéd with Ultrasuede.

Embroidery Stitches

Stem Stitch or the Outline Stitch

- ★ Work this stitch from left to right.
- ★ Mark a line for the length you wish to stitch.
- ★ Come up at A and go down at B, making a straight stitch along the drawn line.
- ★ Emerge at C (which is the midpoint of the previous stitch).
- ★ Keep the thread below the needle point.

This stitch is good for stems and outlines, hence its name.

right-handed

left-handed

Straight Stitch

- ★ Come up at A and go down at B (the desired length of the stitch).
- ★ Pull the thread firmly in place.
- ★ These stitches can be worked evenly or irregularly, and can be varied in length and direction.
- ★ Be sure your stitches are not too long or too loose.

This stitch can be used as an irregular filler stitch.

right-handed

left-handed

Lazy Daisy Stitch

- ★ Come up at A and form a loop, holding the thread down with your thumb.
- ★ Go down at B (close to A, but not into it).
- ★ Emerge at C bringing the needle over the loop of thread.
- ★ Go down at D forming a small anchoring stitch.
- ★ Repeat for multiple petals.

This stitch is a single chain stitch.

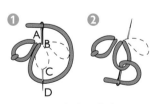

right-handed

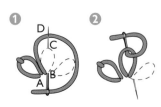

left-handed

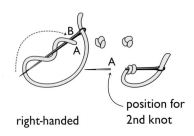

right-handed   position for 2nd knot

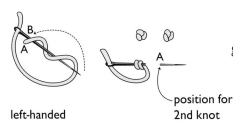

left-handed   position for 2nd knot

French Knot

- ★ Come up at A and wrap the thread 2 or 3 times around the needle.
- ★ Hold the thread taut and go down at B (as close to A as possible, but not into A).
- ★ Hold the knot in place until the needle is completely through the fabric.

French knots are useful in so many ways, either singly sewn or grouped.

Curled Leaf Stitch

- ★ Use silk ribbon and a tapestry needle.
- ★ Come up at A. Make sure the ribbon lies flat on the fabric.
- ★ Pierce the center of the ribbon at B.
- ★ Gently pull the needle through to the back.
- ★ The ribbon edges will curl at the tip.

If the ribbon is pulled too tightly the curled tip disappears into just a point.

You can vary the curled leaf effect by varying the length of the ribbon before piercing it with a needle.

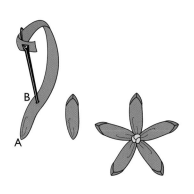

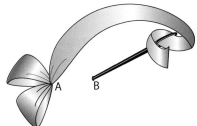

Loop Petals

- ★ Mark a circle as a guide for your stitches.
- ★ Draw the straight lines as points for your petals—3,4,5,6—or simply eyeball the petal placement.
- ★ Come up in the center point of the circle in A and go down at B (the length of the petal).
- ★ Put a round toothpick through the loop to keep its shape while you make the next loop.
- ★ After all the loops are made, add French knots to the center to secure the loops.

Loop petals can be worked singly or grouped.

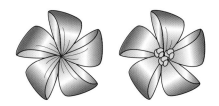

Sewing Instructions for State Flower Blocks

ALABAMA
22nd state—December 14, 1819

21" × 21"
Made and hand quilted by the author
(Pattern and flower, state, and historical information on the CD)

Camellia—the showgirl of the tea family

Design Area	8" square
Block Size	13" × 12"
Wreath Type	Open branch, naturalistic
Techniques	Embroidery, appliqué, broderie perse
Design Source	Inspired by an embroidered piece in an English quilter friend's home

Flower Construction

With wholecloth print leaves and flower plus embroidered stems and petals, this block is easy as pie to make.

★ Use a wholecloth base from a large-scale print flower for the camellia.

★ Trace radiating petals on the print and embroider in a contrasting color for the illusion of multi-petaled blossoms.

★ Make French knots for the center cluster.

★ Embroider the stem with 3 strands of floss.

★ Fussy cut the leaves from a leaf print or a floral fabric to give a realistic effect. Optionally, add a thin layer of batting for a more dimensional effect.

ALASKA
49th state—January 3, 1959

FORGET-ME-NOT
Myosotis alpestris

21" x 21"
Made and hand quilted by the author
(Pattern and flower, state, and historical information on the CD)

Forget-Me-Not—always romantic

Design Area	14" x 12"
Block Size	15" square
Wreath Type	Flower spray
Techniques	Silk ribbon embroidery, appliqué
Design Source	Original

Flower Construction

This is a delicate design that is fun to embroider. Just scatter the blossoms across the field wherever you'd like them to grow. More are always better than less.

★ Use the outline stitch with pearl cotton in variegated green for the embroidered stems.

★ Appliqué the leaves using a variety of batik fabrics.

★ Embroider the flowers using two 5-yard packages of Superior Threads variegated silk ribbon 2mm #120 Bachelor Button or #132 Blue Iris.

★ Use the curled leaf technique for the 5 flower petals.

★ Stitch a single French knot in the center using yellow floss.

ARIZONA
48th state—February 14, 1912

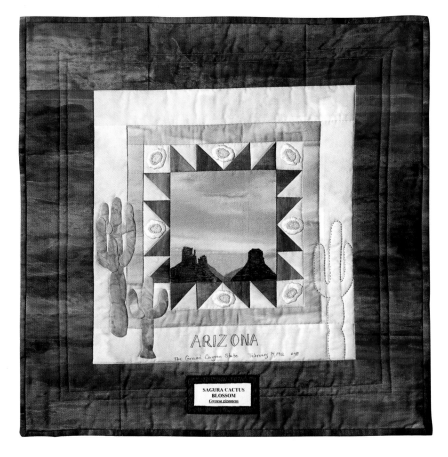

23" × 23"
Made and machine quilted by the author
(Pattern and flower, state, and historical information on the CD)

Sagura Cactus Blossom—short-lived bloom on a long-lived plant

Design Area	11" square
Block Size	15" square
Wreath Type	Traditional pieced cactus block with appliquéd and embroidered blossoms
Techniques	Piecing, floss embroidery, inked drawing
Design Source	Original

*Also spelled Saguaro

Flower Construction

This entire wallhanging is made using hand-painted Skydyes™ fabrics in the colors of the Grand Canyon and sunsets.

★ The centerpiece block is a sunset piece of fabric with a tracing of the natural rock formations, then shaded in with Pigma pen and black Fabrico® marker.

★ Embroider the flowers onto crinoline, then appliqué them in place. To embroider, use the fill-in straight stitch for the outer row using cream or white floss.

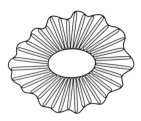

★ Chain stitch the center with yellow floss. Accent the outer portion with dark yellow French knots. Use 2 strands, making 2–3 twists per knot.

★ Trim the crinoline a generous ¼" away from the embroidered blossom.

★ Turn under the stitched edge and appliqué in place. The tucked-under crinoline raw edge will give the blossom a bit of padding and dimension.

ARKANSAS
25th state—June 15, 1836

25" x 25"
Made and hand and machine quilted by the author
(Pattern and flower, state, and historical information on the CD)

Apple Blossom—a sweet smell yields a sweet treat

Design Area   9" square
Block Size   13" square
Wreath Type   Double embroidered circle
Techniques   Silk ribbon embroidery, floss embroidery, appliqué
Design Source   Original

Flower Construction

The process of embroidering all these apple blossoms is slow, but it is satisfying to see the completed beautiful blooms.

★ Trace the wreath circle on your background fabric. Embroider the wreath and stems using Superior Threads variegated silk ribbon 2mm #129 Serengeti.

★ Appliqué the fabric leaves.

★ Draw 1" circles where you would like the blossoms using a light pencil touch. Draw in the 5 petals for each blossom.

★ Embroider the blossoms with white embroidery floss using a fill-in straight stitch at a slight angle on the diagonal.

★ Outline the petals with the outline stitch. If it is easier for you to fill in an enclosed area, then sew the outline stitch first. This delineates the petals.

★ Add a yellow French knot in the center using embroidery floss.

★ Add linear accents using one strand of light pink embroidery floss radiating out from the center.

CALIFORNIA
31st state—September 9, 1850

22" x 22"
Made and hand quilted by the author
(Pattern and flower, state, and historical information on the CD)

Golden Poppy—the essence of the California good life

Design Area	12" x 11"
Block Size	15" square
Wreath Type	Open wreath with landscape center
Techniques	Appliqué, ribbon appliqué
Design Source	Original

Flower Construction

A landscape center is surrounded by golden poppies created by appliqué and ribbon work.

★ For the fabric poppies, cut a variety of golden yellow fabric prints and shades for the petals and appliqué in place.

★ For the ribbon poppies, use 8" lengths of #9 (1½" wide) wired ribbon per blossom to create a gathered length of ribbon. You will need 1 yard of ribbon.

★ Secure the gathers by wrapping the wires around the two ends.

★ Bring the ends together and form a flat circle. Sew the seam.

★ Position the poppies on crinoline and stitch the center opening down, forming a tight oval.

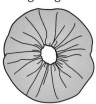

★ Fold the bottom portion of the ribbon over the top portion, forming a cup-shaped flower. Because the ribbon has wire in it, you can sculpt this cup to form a pleasing poppy shape.

★ Once you are satisfied with your blossom's shape, secure the edges on the crinoline, place it in position on the wreath, and stitch it in place.

★ Make a bow with ½ yard of #3 (¾" wide) ombré blue ribbon and appliqué it in place.

COLORADO
38th state—August 1, 1876

23" x 24"
Made and hand quilted by the author
(Pattern and flower, state, and historical information on the CD)

Rocky Mountain Columbine—delicate beauty a mile high

Design Area	10" square
Block Size	14" square
Wreath Type	Open wreath frame with landscape center
Techniques	Appliqué, ribbon work
Design Source	Original

Flower Construction

The majestic Rocky Mountains of Colorado are the inspiration for a landscape center surrounded by a wreath of columbine.

Block

★ Trace the wreath circle onto the background fabric and cut out a circle on the line.

★ Construct your landscape and layer it under the circle opening.

★ Baste and stitch to hold all the elements in place.

★ Accent the wreath with 5 columbines made in 3 different sizes.

★ Add 3 side view flowers at the tips of the wreath.

★ Ink details to depict stems, leaves, and buds.

Flowers

★ Use #9 (1½" wide) solid purple wire-edged ribbon for the pointy petals for the base of each columbine blossom. You will need 3 yards.

★ Cut 5 strips for each flower, for a total of 35, from the template on the CD. Remove the wire from the narrow edge of each piece of ribbon.

(Continued on page 22)

COLORADO

★ Fold the wired ribbon edge down to the unwired narrower bottom edge forming a sharp tip. Pin to hold together.

★ Stitch across the bottom of five petals and gather tightly.

★ Stitch each 1½" section of ribbon in the square U technique. If using wire-edged ribbon, remove the wire from the bottom stitched edge.

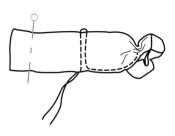

★ Form a circle and secure on a square of crinoline.

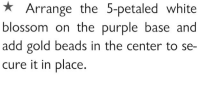

Note: when gathering the petals for the smaller columbine, gather up from the bottom edge about ¼" so the resulting petal is smaller in size.

★ The 5-petaled white portion of the flower is made with #5 (1" wide) ribbon, using 9" per flower, so 2 yards of ribbon are needed. Make these with either wire-edged or unwired ribbon. If unwired, the petals are softer and uncontrollable.

★ Arrange the 5-petaled white blossom on the purple base and add gold beads in the center to secure it in place.

★ For the upper ½ flowers, use 3 purple petals and 3 white "square u" petals.

CONNECTICUT

5th state—January 9, 1788

21" x 21"
Made and machine quilted by the author
(Pattern and flower, state, and historical information on the CD)

Mountain Laurel—lovely but deadly

Design Area   11½" square
Block Size   13" square
Wreath Type   Closed circle with clusters of flowers at compass points
Techniques   Appliqué, origami flowers
Design Source Original

Flower Construction

This wreath features appliqué with dimensional origami folded fabric flowers.

★ Cut 1" x 1" squares of tone-on-tone white or off-white fabric. Use several different fabrics for variety.

★ Make a ½" hexagon template from plastic. Very lightly trace the hexagon shape in the center of the fabric.

★ Fold the fabric over to the back along the drawn lines.

★ Secure the folds with a bead in the center and several anchoring stitches.

★ Make 24–30 folded hexagons per flower. This is a slow process but not hard and the end result is worth the effort.

★ Arrange the folded hexagons on a crinoline base with a hidden stitch through the center of the flower using white thread. Overlap the hexagons to hide the crinoline base.

★ With a #01 Pigma pen, very lightly draw 5 or 6 radiating lines from the center outward, not touching the outer edge of the folded flowerette.

★ Trim away the excess crinoline and arrange the flowers on the leafy wreath. For the leaves, use a solid, dark-green polished cotton or chintz and a batik for contrast.

DELAWARE
1st state—December 7, 1787

22" × 23"
Made and machine quilted by the author
(Pattern and flower, state, and historical information on the CD)

*Peach Blossom—the flower of an old fruit
for the oldest state*

Design Area	9" square
Block Size	13" square
Wreath Type	Closed circular wreath
Techniques	Appliqué, silk ribbon embroidery, floss embroidery
Design Source	Original

Flower Construction

This is a bias stem wreath with embroidered branches and silk ribbon embroidered flowers. You can add more blossoms if you want a more bountiful look. They are fun to make! You won't be able to stop embroidering these petals and leaves.

★ Appliqué the main stem with fabric cut on the bias. Use pearl cotton to embroider the side branches with an outline stitch.

★ Embroider the flowers with Superior Threads variegated silk ribbon 7mm #109 Begonia. The sample has 20 flowers inside the wreath and 32 outside. To make the same, you will need 6 packages @ 3 yards per package. The variegated ribbon adds lots of variation to the petals' coloring.

★ Make 5 petals for each flower using the curled leaf stitch. The diameter of the flower is about ¾". Add a gold bead in the center.

★ Scatter the blossoms on the branches around the stem in a pleasing manner.

★ Stitch the leaves with the same technique using Superior Threads variegated silk ribbon 7mm #113 Soft Green.

FLORIDA
27th state—March 3, 1845

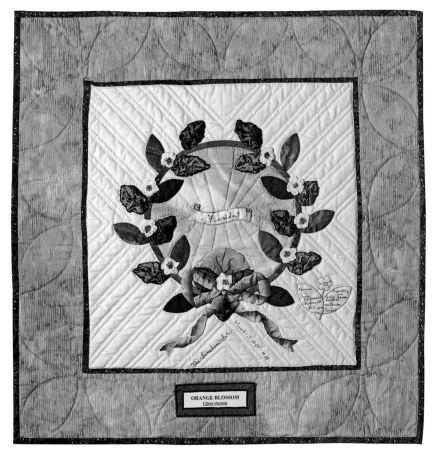

22" × 23"
Made and hand quilted by the author
(Pattern and flower, state, and historical information on the CD)

Orange Blossom—a bridal bouquet favorite

Design Area	12" square
Block Size	14" × 15"
Wreath Type	Closed circle with dimensional ribbon flowers and gathered ribbon leaves
Technique	Dimensional appliqué
Design Source	Original

Flower Construction

You can almost smell the orange blossoms and feel the sunshine as you stitch this wreath.

★ The leaves in the wreath are a combination of ribbon and fabric. Use an assortment of green fabrics for a varied effect. For ribbon leaves you will need 1 yard of #9 (1½" wide) wired ribbon. Cut 3" of ribbon per leaf. See directions on the CD for Guam's bougainvillea for gathering the ribbon into leaves.

★ Make 9 blossoms. Use 6" of #3 (¾" wide) wired or unwired ribbon per blossom. You will need 1½ to 2 yards. Follow the stitching pattern for the square U technique. Use spacing of 1¼" per petal. Be sure to include a ½" margin at either end. Form a closed circle of gathered petals, stitch together, and place on a square of crinoline.

★ Pad the center opening with excess ribbon tails and heavily bead the center. Add French knots of embroidery floss for additional texture and dimension.

★ The centerpiece orange can be made from a gathered piece of wide orange ribbon or a piece of orange fabric.

★ Make a real bow from 1 yard of 1" wide blue ribbon, arrange it at the base of the wreath, and anchor it in place. This is the easiest way to make an "appliquéd" bow.

GEORGIA

4th state—January 2, 1788

24" x 24"
Made and hand quilted by the author
(Pattern and flower, state, and historical information on the CD)

Cherokee Rose—beautiful symbol of a sad story

Design Area	13" square
Block Size	17" x 16"
Wreath Type	Open circle against a blue sky background with 4 compass-point flowers
Technique	Appliqué
Design Source	Original

Flower Construction

This wreath is elegant in its simplicity. You can add four more roses for a fuller wreath. Sashiko-embroidered leaves complete the wreath.

★ Make templates for each of the 3 sizes of petals.

★ Trace the templates on the right side of the fabric. The drawn line represents the sewing line. Cut an assortment of petals from a stripey white fabric or an off-white print for a realistic effect.

★ Arrange the petals randomly. Stitch the petals on a tear-away foundation base, then place them on the background fabric for final sewing.

★ Pad the center with a layer of batting and embroider 2 rows of French knots around the center.

★ Quilt in shadow leaves to give the illusion of a full wreath.

HAWAII

50th state—August 21, 1959

25" x 25"
Made and hand quilted by the author
(Pattern and flower, state, and historical information on the CD)

Yellow Hibiscus /Pua Aloalo — endangered but thriving

Design Area	12" square
Block Size	14" square
Wreath Type	Crescent wreath with landscape center
Techniques	Appliqué, ribbon work
Design Source	Original

Flower Construction

This landscape wreath was created for a class I taught at Quilt Hawaii in Waikiki Beach, Honolulu, several years ago. The classroom windows were facing Diamond Head with the blue Pacific Ocean in front of it. The view was an inspiring sight for the class project.

For ribbon flowers:

★ Cut 12" lengths of #9 (1½" wide) red or golden yellow wire-edged ribbon. You will need 1 yard. Expose the wire from both ends of the cut edges. Hold the wire and gently slide the ribbon toward the middle. Gather as tightly as possible WITHOUT breaking the wire. If you do break it, you'll have to gather with a needle and thread.

★ Secure the gathers by wrapping the wires around the two ends.

★ Bring the ends together and form a flat circle. Sew the seam.

(Continued on page 28)

Hawaii

★ Using doubled thread, stitch an X pattern in the center opening, closing the circle opening.

★ Before the opening is completely closed, insert a prepared center stamen into the center opening exposing about 1½" and secure with extra stitches.

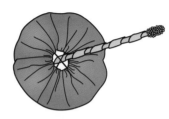

★ To make the center stamen, tightly roll a 4" length of #3 (¾" wide) red wire-edged ribbon lengthwise toward either the light side or the dark side and twist to hold the rolls in place. You will need ½ yard.

★ Tie one end into a knot and trim the excess frayed ribbon.

★ Cover this tip with gold beads. They may be sewn on one at a time or the tip may be dipped in glue and rolled in beads for speedier production.

Optional: The outer rim of the bloom may be crinkled for a more natural look. Crease into 5 petals.

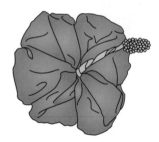

For fabric flowers:

★ For fabric hibiscus, cut petals from yellow and red fabrics and appliqué them on a base of tear-away foundation. Position on the wreath and sew in place. You can also fussy cut wholecloth hibiscus from tropical print fabric.

IDAHO
43rd state—July 3, 1890

22" x 22"
Made by the author and machine quilted by Ellen Peters
(Pattern and flower, state, and historical information on the CD)

Mock Orange—a great imitator

Design Area	11" square
Block Size	14" square
Wreath Type	Circle
Techniques	Silk ribbon embroidery, sashiko
Design Source	Classic circle wreath

Flower Construction

This perfect circle wreath is a classic and easy to create with two simple techniques.

★ Use Superior Threads silk ribbon 2mm #131 Vine to embroider the wreath stem using the outline stitch for the main stem and side branches.

★ Group the flowers in clusters of three.

★ Use ¼" wide ribbon and stitch in the square U technique with 1¼" petal spacing. If you would like a fuller petal, use 1½" spacing. For 6" flowers, you will need 6 yards.

★ Use the sashiko embroidery stitch next to appliquéd leaves to create shadow leaves. This gives the illusion of more leaves with less work and fabric.

ILLINOIS
21st state—December 3, 1818

21" × 21"
Made by the author and machine quilted by Ellen Peters
(Pattern and flower, state, and historical information on the CD)

Violet—the children's favorite

Design Area	8" square
Block Size	14" square
Wreath Type	Circle
Techniques	Appliqué, silk ribbon work, embroidery
Design Source	Traditional wreath shape

Flower Construction

This wreath is made of appliquéd leaves with ruched silk violets. Use 1 yard of two different shades of Hanah 1" wide bias silk purple ribbon for the flowers—a dark purple and a light lilac shade for contrast—or 1½ yards of #9 (1½" wide) ribbon.

★ Appliqué heart-shaped leaves in a circle for the wreath base. Outline them with an embroidered outline stitch using a black and gold metallic DMC thread to define the leaves with a bit of sparkle. If you can't find this brand of thread, try twisting one strand each of black and metallic gold to see if you get the desired effect.

★ This is the simplest ruched technique to make as you only need to stitch 3 triangles to form a flower. Use 3" of #5 (1" wide) ribbon per violet. Make 12 violets. If using #9 (1½" wide) ribbon, use 4½" per flower; you'll need 1½ yards of bias silk ribbon.

★ Fold the ribbon in half and put a pin in the crease. Fold the ribbon in half again and pin again in the creases. These are guideposts for your stitching pattern.

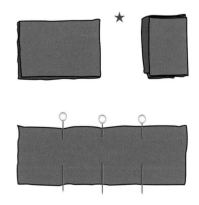

(Continued on page 31)

ILLINOIS

★ With wire-edged ribbon, you need to trim off the tails to about ¼". Be careful you do not trim too close to the stitched petals or you'll have trouble with the next step.

★ Tuck the tails behind the flower and secure with a few stitches. Pick up a bead while taking these stitches and you accomplish two jobs with one stitch.

Unfold the ribbon. Stitch a ruching pattern, taking care to loop the thread over the top and bottom of the selvage edge when changing stitching directions. Gently gather as tightly as possible and secure with backstitches.

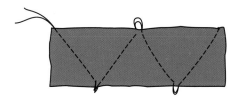

★ When using basic silk ribbon your violet is complete at this step. Simply add a bead or two to the center and you have a finished violet.

INDIANA
19th state—December 11, 1816

18" × 18"
Made and hand and machine quilted by the author
(Pattern and flower, state, and historical information on the CD)

Flower Construction

Fussy cut fabric from a large-scale floral and use inventive piecing to mimic nature's art.

★ Piece the 4 blocks using a large-scale floral print.

★ Set the blocks on point; the top block represents a full blown peony with all the petals a dark color. The 2 side flowers represent a peony partially opened with a pair of green leaves. The lower block represents a peony bud with 2 pairs of green leaves and center flower petals.

★ Embroider the connecting stems and appliqué the leaves in position. Embroider the stem with Superior Threads variegated 2mm #115 Forest Green.

Peony—long-lived and sweet to people and insects

Design Area	8" square
Block Size	12" square
Wreath Type	Pieced
Techniques	Piecing, appliqué, floss embroidery
Design Source	Traditional pieced block

IOWA

29th state—December 28, 1846

24" x 24"
Made and hand quilted by the author and machine quilted by Ellen Peters
(Pattern and flower, state, and historical information on the CD)

Wild Prairie Rose—simple beauty in abundance

Design Area	13" x 9"
Block Size	17" square
Wreath Type	Naturalistic sprawling branch
Techniques	Appliqué, floss embroidery, Ultrasuede appliqué
Design Source	Inspired from a photo of a quilt, maker unknown

Flower Construction

Skydyes fabrics are used almost entirely in this piece, from the assorted pink petals to the hand-painted background fabric to the border. An assortment of green fabrics is used for the leaves. Ultrasuede is appliquéd for the bud cases with a bit of batting for padding.

This block is a slow-sew, but not hard. It is very beautiful and you can almost reach down and pick a blossom up as you walk along the prairie. You will be very happy when the last leaf is sewn in place.

★ Trace the stems onto the background fabric and draw light guide lines for leaf placement.

★ Embroider the stems.

★ Begin sewing the leaves on. This will take a little while, so make a few roses in between sewing leaf clusters.

★ Make the rose by sewing petals on a base of tear-away stabilizer.

★ Position the roses on the leaf cluster and appliqué in place.

KANSAS

34th state—January 29, 1861

23" × 23"
Made and hand quilted by the author and machine quilted by Ellen Peters
(Pattern and flower, state, and historical information on the CD)

Sunflower—golden abundance on the prairie

Design Area	8" square
Block Size	14" square
Wreath Type	A 4-block set with a center opening
Techniques	Piecing, appliqué
Design Source	Variation on a traditional pieced block

Flower Construction

This is a traditionally pieced sunflower block with a variation of appliquéd petals. It was great fun stitching this sunny block during a cold New England winter.

★ Piece the 4 blocks using a variety of golden yellow fabrics for the many petals.

★ Appliqué the overlapping petals on top of the pieced blocks.

★ Add a brown circular center with a bit of batting underneath.

★ Sew the 4 blocks together and add an inner border strip with a wreath of appliquéd sunflower leaves.

★ Add prairie points instead of traditional binding to mimic the flower petals of the sunflower and rays of sunshine.

Kentucky

15th state*—June 1, 1792
***One of four commonwealths in the nation**

21" x 21"
Made by the author and machine quilted by Ellen Peters
(Pattern and flower, state, and historic information on the CD)

Goldenrod—not the allergy culprit it's cracked up to be

Design Area	10" square
Block Size	14" square
Wreath Type	Paper-cut square wreath with cornerstone blossoms placed on the diagonal
Technique	Layered appliqué
Design Source	Traditional fleur-de-lis album block design with an original abstract twist

Flower Construction

Use a variety of shades and prints of golden yellow fabrics for the layered appliqué. Use gold metallic thread for the embroidered accent between the petals (outline stitch) and for the accents around the entire flower head (French knots). The nylon core prevents fraying.

★ Begin with the largest layer first and proceed upward to the smallest layer as the last to be appliquéd.

★ Appliqué the largest layer onto a piece of fabric for the next layer.

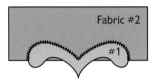

★ Trace the second layer onto this fabric after the first layer is appliquéd. Trim to the seam allowance.

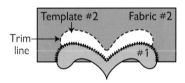

★ Place the third layer of fabric underneath the second layer and appliqué in place. Trace the next layer onto this piece of fabric.

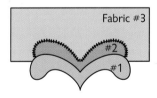

★ Embroider between the layers with gold metallic thread.

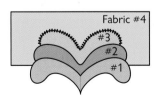

LOUISIANA

18th state—April 30, 1812

21" x 21"
Made and hand quilted by the author
(Pattern and flower, state, and historical information on the CD)

*Magnolia—splendid fragrance in a tree
the dinosaurs knew*

Design Area	8" square
Block Size	11" square
Wreath type	Embroidered square wreath
Techniques	Floss embroidery, appliqué
Design Source	Inspired by a quilting stencil

Flower Construction

This block is a simple, yet elegant design.

★ Trace the outline of the leafy wreath on the background fabric using a light box or transfer paper.

★ Embroider with 2 strands of floss in a pleasing shade of green to complement and contrast with your background fabric. You can use 2 different shades of green or a variegated green floss for interest.

★ Cut the centerpiece flower as one piece; add about ¼" beyond the drawn stitching line.

★ Add a layer of wool or other thin batting under the flower, cutting the batting a bit smaller than the flower's shape.

★ Appliqué in place.

★ Embroider and quilt the petals at the same time to give the flower a dimensional effect. Use 2 different shades of cream and ecru for contrast embroidery.

MAINE
23rd state—March 15, 1820

22" x 22"
Made and hand quilted by the author
(Pattern and flower, state, and historical information on the CD)

White Pine Tree Tassel and Cones—stylish form and function

Design Area	10" x 11"
Block Size	13" x 14"
Wreath Type	Asymmetrical L-shaped crescent
Techniques	Appliqué, ribbon work, floss embroidery
Design Source	Original interpretation of a traditional design; inspired by the Wild Rose block pattern *(Carrie Hall Blocks* by Bettina Havig, AQS, 1999)

Flower Construction

Appliquéd bias stems with embroidered pine needles, a chickadee, and dimensional pine cones from wire-edged ribbon make this vintage crescent wreath.

Pine Cone

★ Cut 26" of #5 (1" wide) wire-edged ombré brownish ribbon into 2" strips. Remove the wire from the lighter-colored side of the ribbon.

★ Fold the ribbon in half with the 2 cut edges together. Pinch the wired fold edge.

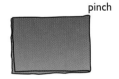

★ Unfold and fold the wired edge down to the center. Pin to hold in place.

★ Stitch across the bottom with doubled quilting thread. Gather tightly to form a "tent" shaped pine cone scale. Make 6 scales per cone.

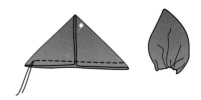

(Continued on page 38)

MAINE

★ Draw a cone shape on crinoline. Arrange the scales from the tip to the base (stem end) making sure all raw edges are hidden. Secure the scales with hidden stitches using matching thread. Trim away the excess crinoline and stitch the cone in place on background fabric. Secure in place.

★ Use the last 2" of ribbon to form a twisted stem for one of the pine cones.

Chickadee

★ Construct the chickadee as a layered appliqué, as an embroidery, or color it in with Fabrico markers.

Pine Needles

★ Embroider the needles with a single strand of dark green or forest green embroidery floss using the outline stitch.

★ Embroider the base of the needle clusters with brown floss using the straight stitch.

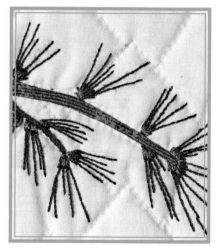

MARYLAND

7th state—April 28, 1788

22" x 22"
Made and hand quilted by the author
(Pattern and flower, state, and historical information on the CD)

Black-eyed Susan—uncommonly common beauty

Design Area	11" square
Block Size	14" square
Wreath Type	A square paper-cut wreath
Techniques	Ultrasuede appliqué, floss embroidery
Design Source	Inspired by an 1849 Baltimore Album, quiltmaker unknown. It was thought to have been made for Thomas Lewis Darnell when he married Adelaine Virginia Bartnoff.

Flower Construction

The wreath stems can be appliquéd, embroidered, or made with a thin strip of Ultrasuede.

★ Make a template and cut petals from Ultrasuede.

★ Stitch the inner portion of the petals that abut each other on a crinoline base to form a flower unit. The center disk needs a bit of padding before stitching down the flower center. Trim away the excess crinoline.

★ Position the flowers on background fabric. Stitch the remaining portion of the petals in place with tiny stitches using matching thread.

★ Embroider around the petals using the outline stitch with 1 strand of embroidery floss in a matching color.

MASSACHUSETTS

6th state*—February 6, 1788
*One of four commonwealths in the nation

21" × 21"
Made and hand and machine quilted by the author
(Pattern and flower, state, and historical information on the CD)

Mayflower—symbol of resurgence

Design Area   11" square
Block Size   12½" square
Wreath Type   Traditional closed circle
Techniques   Appliqué, dimensional appliqué
Design Source   Original

Flower Construction

A classic technique is perfect for this delicate flower.

★ Use 7" of #3 (¾" wide) un-wired satin ribbon per blossom; you'll need 4 yards total. If you use wire-edged ribbon, remove the wire from both edges of the ribbon before beginning to stitch.

★ Starting ½" in from the cut edge, stitch zigzag open triangles at 1" intervals along the length of the ribbon to form 8 petals on the outer edge. Be sure a loop of thread lies over the top and bottom edges of the ribbon before continuing to stitch down the diagonal sides of the triangles. This loop allows the thread to gather easily without knotting.

★ Gather your thread every 2 or 3 triangles to prevent the thread from tangling. This technique is known as ruching. Bring the ends together to form a circle of petals. Secure the end petals together.

★ Stitch the tips of the inner petals into a common center on a crinoline base.

★ Make 17 or 18 flowers. Add a French knot in the center using 3 wraps with 3 strands of yellow floss. Attach to the wreath with hidden stitches.

MICHIGAN

26th state—January 26, 1837

25" x 25"
Made and machine quilted by the author
(Pattern and flower, state, and historical information on the CD)

Apple Blossom—fragrant and fruitful

Design Area 10" x 9"
Block Size 15" square
Wreath Type Tree-shaped
Techniques Floss embroidery, paint
Design Source Original

Flower Construction

This is an embroidered wreath base with appliquéd leaves and painted apple blossoms. Use acrylic white paint; my brush of choice is a round Loew-Cornell brush size 6. Practice on scrap fabric until you master your petal-painting technique.

Tip: Turn the fabric to make each petal rather than turning your hand and brush as this may vary the brush strokes.

You might want to draw light pencil circles for a guide to painting the 5 petals. This is really not necessary if you just practice a while. It won't take much practice before you have mastered the petal-painting technique. In no time at all you'll be painting up an orchard full of blossoms and having too much fun!

★ Start on the outside of the petal and brush toward the center having a fairly full brush. Load the brush with paint and push down on the brush to form the tip of the petal, then pull up to form the narrow center of the petal.

★ Paint 5 petals. Let dry completely before proceeding to the next step.

★ To highlight the center of the petals use a dry brush technique, i.e., the brush is brushed off on paper toweling until almost no paint remains on it—just enough to give a light tint to the petal. Let dry. The centers are toothpick dots of yellow paint.

★ Use fabric print leaves to give a realistic effect to your painted blossoms.

MINNESOTA

32nd state—May 11, 1858

25" × 25"
Made and hand and machine quilted by the author
(Pattern and flower, state, and historical information on the CD)

Pink & White Lady's Slipper—queenly, sensitive, and rare

Design Area	10" square
Block Size	16" square
Wreath Type	Paper-cut base with flowers and leaves on the diagonal
Techniques	Appliqué, Ultrasuede appliqué
Design Source	Original

Flower Construction

A 4-diamond pattern is the center of the wreath, which is made of appliquéd leaves.

★ Place the flowers at the diagonal points of the wreath.

★ The petals of the lady slipper are a combination of pink fabrics and white Ultrasuede.

★ Embroider around the Ultrasuede for contrast.

★ Use a folded origami hexagon (see Connecticut's mountain laurel) as a base for the yellow French knots for the flower's center.

MISSISSIPPI

20th state—December 10, 1817

MAGNOLIA
Magnolia grandiflora

13" x 13"
Made and hand and machine quilted by the author
(Pattern and flower, state, and historical information on the CD)

Magnolia—ancient magnificence

Design Area	9" square
Block Size	13" square
Wreath Type	Pieced block with appliquéd center medallion
Techniques	Piecing, appliqué
Design Source	Traditional pieced block

Flower Construction

This is an elegant pieced block in black and white symbolizing a formal black tie affair and celebrating an elegant flower. You might not be able to stop with just one block! This design would make an exquisite quilt of any size.

★ Piece together the four 4" blocks.

★ Connect the blocks to each other with 2" sashing.

★ Appliqué a wholecloth magnolia with a layer of wool backing for the center blossom.

★ Delineate the petals with outline embroidery that penetrates the wool batting for an indented effect.

★ Fill the center with thin wool French knots for added texture and interest.

MISSOURI

24th state—August 10, 1821

20" × 20"
Made and hand and machine quilted by the author
(Pattern and more information on the CD)

Hawthorn—sturdy and delicious

Design Area	8½" square
Block Size	11" square
Wreath Type	Crossed branches
Techniques	Appliqué, silk ribbon embroidery
Design Source	Traditional crossed branches from album quilts

Flower Construction

This crossed branch wreath is appliquéd with silk ribbon embroidered flowers and red berries. It includes an inked detail of the Gateway Arch, a St. Louis Landmark, on the inner wreath area.

★ Draw a ⅜" circle with a light pencil where you would like your flowers.

★ Stitch 5 lazy daisy stitches with white silk ribbon, radiating out from the center point.

★ Use yellow embroidery floss for the flower center.

★ Use 1 to 2 twists of Superior Threads variegated silk ribbon 4mm #126 Cana Lily for French knots for each of the berries. You will need 2 packages.

MONTANA
41st state—November 8, 1889

19" × 19"

Made and hand quilted by the author and machine quilted by Ellen Peters
(Pattern and flower, state, and historical information on the CD)

Bitterroot—valuable hardiness in a land of wealth

Design Area	6½" square
Block Size	10" × 12"
Wreath Type	Simple circle
Technique	Fabrico markers
Design Source	Original

Flower Construction

This delicate, early spring flower is at home on a gravelly riverbank or in this wreath.

★ Draw the wreath circles using a 1½" diameter circle. Use a hard lead pencil that will erase on fabric and make light marks. Test on a piece of scrap fabric.

★ Draw eight 1½" circles evenly around the circle and mark the center point of each circle. Now mark the flowers' petals. This is really easier than it looks.

★ Lightly draw the first 4 petals at right angles to each other. Next fill in petals on either side of the first 4 petals. Finally draw petal tips on either side of those petals.

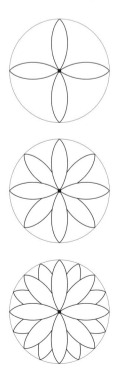

(Continued on page 46)

MONTANA

★ Trace over the outline of the petals with a fine black marker.

★ Shade in the petals with #106 Lipstick Pink from the tip to the center, leaving the center light in color. Use #115 Cherry Pink for dark streaky shading.

★ Use a brown ink #01 Pigma pen for linear and dot accents at the base of each petal.

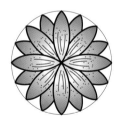

★ The pieced border is a 1" x 2" rectangle with a 1" square stitched on the diagonal on either end. Trim and fold over for a Flying Geese strip.

★ Draw and color in 5 petals in the center of the strip.

Note: A hand-painted Skydyes fabric was used to represent the gravel river beds where this plant grows.

NEBRASKA

37th state—March 1, 1867

19" × 19"
Made and hand quilted by the author
(Pattern and flower, state, and historical information on the CD)

Goldenrod—maligned wildflower deserving of a better reputation

Design Area 9" square
Block Size 12" square
Wreath Type 5 plumes swirl inward around a circular base
Techniques Silk ribbon embroidery, floss embroidery, appliqué
Design Source Original

Flower Construction

Embroidery brings the appliqué to life in this quilt.

★ Draw a 6½" circle and place 5 swirling plumes along the circle.

★ Embroider the main stem in an outline stitch with Superior Threads variegated silk ribbon 2mm #131 Vine. You will need one 5-yard package.

★ Use 2 strands of green floss to outline stitches for the side branches (1).

★ Embroider branches off the plumes in variegated yellow floss with the chain stitch (2).

★ Fill in the branches with Superior Thread variegated silk ribbon 2mm #106 Sunflower. You will need three 5-yard packages. Using the curled leaf stitch, make petals along the length on both sides of the branch (3).

★ Fill in between the petals with French knots using 3 twists. Making the knots from floss adds contrasting texture to the silk ribbon petals (4).

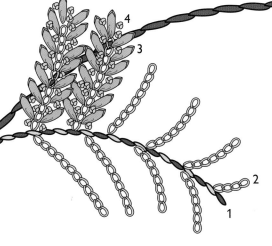

NEVADA

36th state—October 31, 1864

18" x 18"
Made and hand and machine quilted by the author
(Pattern and flower, state, and historical information on the CD)

Sagebrush—homely, hardy, useful, and fragrant

Design Area	11" square with 6" center wreath
Block Size	11" square
Wreath Type	Simple circle
Technique	Floss embroidery
Design Source	Original

Flower Construction

This is a gentle and delicate block that is a bit slow to sew with all the embroidery, but it is very pleasant and satisfying to work on. The border fabric is a unique hand-painted Skydyes block design.

★ Outline stitch the main stem using Madeira silk floss #1707 dark blue gray. Use 2 strands for the circle outline (1).

★ Use a single strand of Madeira silk floss #1708 for the branches off the main stem using the outline stitch (2).

★ Use 2 strands of Madeira silk floss #1802 for the petals using a lazy daisy stitch (3).

★ Use 2 strands of the same #1802 floss for French knots at the tips of the branches (4).

★ Fill in the inner corner areas of the block with the same stitches in a sagebrush design.

★ Enhance the area between the embroideries with quilting, which forms a secondary pattern like a golden wreath around the center embroidery.

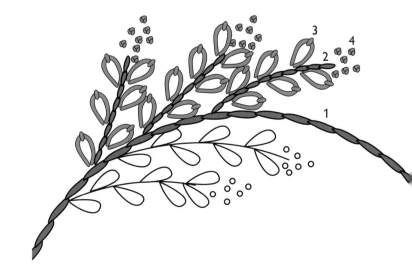

NEW HAMPSHIRE

9th state—June 21, 1788

24" x 24"
Made and hand and machine quilted by the author
(*Pattern and flower, state, and historical information on the CD*)

Lilac—hardy, long-lived romance

Design Area	13" x 11"
Block Size	15" square
Wreath Type	Partially opened circle
Techniques	Appliqué, ribbon work
Design Source	Original interpretation of a traditional shape

Flower Construction

You'll need 2 yards of ombré purple wire-edged ribbon size #5 (1" wide) for these easy-to-make crushed lilacs.

★ Cut the ribbon into 3 pieces: 36", 24", and 12" long.

★ Draw the lilac shapes onto crinoline.

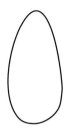

★ Use a double length of quilting thread and sew a running stitch about ¼" in length down the middle of the ribbon.

★ Gather the thread gently, swirling and twirling the ribbon as you pull. Arrange onto the drawn lilac shape.

★ Flatten the ribbon in place and secure it to the crinoline with hidden stitches. Trim away the excess crinoline. *Optional: add beads in scattered spots to represent the floret centers.*

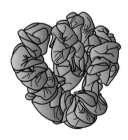

★ Repeat with the remaining ribbon for 2 more blooms. Position them on the background fabric and secure in place with hidden stitches.

NEW JERSEY
3rd state—December 18, 1787

21" x 20"
Made by the author and machine quilted by Ellen Peters
(Pattern and flower, state, and historical information on the CD)

Violet—pretty, edible, and perennial

Design Area   10" square
Block Size   14" square
Wreath Type   Closed circle
Techniques   Appliqué, floss embroidery
Design Source   Original

Flower Construction

The wreath is made up of 3 different violets with a total of 15 flowers. They are embroidered using a variety of purple threads for contrast in textures and shading, and outlined with black. Bias stems are used for the wreath circle with appliquéd leaves in 2 different sizes.

★ For the flowers, use a fill-in or chevron stitch. Some of the petals are two-toned with light purple on one side and a medium tone on the other. You will need Superior Threads King Tut quilting thread—4 strands of variegated purple #938 and #948, 1 strand of purple embroidery floss, and pearl cotton.

★ Use 1 strand of black embroidery floss for the outline embroidery around each of the flowers for an enhanced effect.

★ No flower center is shown, but add one if you like.

NEW MEXICO
47th state—January 6, 1912

21" × 24"
Made and hand and machine quilted by the author
(Pattern and flower, state, and historical information on the CD)

Yucca Flower—utility and beauty

Design Area	6" × 9"
Block Size	12" × 15"
Wreath Type	Embroidered plant in an oval frame set against a hand-painted Skydyes sunset fabric
Technique	Floss embroidery
Design Source	Original

Flower Construction

This was the last state flower I designed. It gave me great difficulty for a long period of time as I could not come up with a suitable wreath design to my liking. Finally, it dawned on me not to design a wreath but rather to use the entire magnificent plant in all its blooming glory. So that is just what I did. I tied a beautiful flowing bow around the stalk as a giant celebration of its natural beauty. After that, everything fell into place with this simple yet elegant design framed in an oval opening. This design was slow to embroider, but lots of fun in stitching and watching it grow with each sewing session.

★ Trace the outline of the plant leaves on your background fabric.

★ Embroider the leaves by outlining with a single strand of floss, then complete with a diagonal fill-in stitch.

★ Use ivory pearl cotton for the embroidered stalk and silk ivory buttonhole twist for the side branches.

★ Use an open lazy daisy stitch with 3 strands of floss for the flowers and fill in with a small, open lazy daisy stitch.

★ Using the same floss, scatter French knots over the plant for texture and contrast.

★ Embroider a ribbon on the stalk and also tie a real one of variegated narrow or 7mm silk ribbon and stitch in place.

NEW YORK
11th state—July 26, 1788

19" x 16"
Made and hand and machine quilted by the author
(Pattern and flower, state, and historical information on the CD)

Rose—popular, scented, at home in town and country

Design Area	19" x 16"
Block Size	19" x 16"
Wreath Type	Implied
Techniques	Ink work with Pigma pen, broderie perse, embroidery
Design Source	Inspired by a design in *Treasury of Flower Designs* by Susan Garber, Dover Publications (1981)

Flower Construction

This is a rectangular inked wreath with broderie perse cornerstone flowers. The result is elegant yet simple.

★ Trace the wreath details on your background fabric using a light box and a hard lead mechanical pencil or transfer paper.

★ Back the fabric with freezer paper or cover with masking tape.

★ Refer to page 11 for instructions on inking.

★ Select 4 roses and leaves from a fabric print and appliqué as broderie perse cornerstones.

Options: Add a thin layer of batting to the roses for a padded effect. Instead of inking the leaves, they can be embroidered.

NORTH CAROLINA
12th state—November 21, 1789

19" x 19"
Made and hand quilted by the author
(Pattern and flower, state, and historical information on the CD)

Dogwood—an ornamental treat

Design Area	7" square
Block Size	13" square
Wreath Type	Classic branch
Techniques	Appliqué, silk embroidery
Design Source	Antique album wreath

Flower Construction

This block is a traditional Baltimore Album pattern and is unique in its asymmetrical appearance.

Embroider the stem using an outline stitch and a curled leaf stitch with Superior Threads variegated silk ribbon 2mm #129 Serengeti. You will need one 5-yard package.

★ Stitch the stem with 2 rows of outline stitching that flares at the base of the stem.

★ Fill the flared area with the curled leaf stitch.

★ Appliqué leaves and petals. Use a variety of ecru prints in the petals.

★ Embroider French knots to fill the centers.

NORTH DAKOTA
39th state—November 2, 1889

24" × 24"
Made and machined quilted by the author
(Pattern and flower, state, and historical information on the CD)

Wild Prairie Rose—hardy and tasty

Design Area	12" square
Block Size	15" square
Wreath Type	Twisted branches
Technique	Appliqué
Design Source	Original

Flower Construction

This appliquéd wreath features the wild prairie rose from bud to full bloom and a stylized bluebird.

★ Line the 5 petals with a contrasting fabric. Sew petals to the lining and turn them inside out.

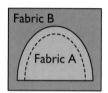

★ Turn in the bottom edge, stitch it closed, then gather along the closed edge.

★ Stitch all 5 petals together. Gather to make a flower.

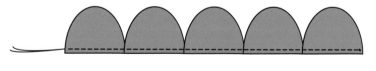

(Continued on page 55)

NORTH DAKOTA

★ Make center stamens of yellow wool cut and tied together in a loose bundle and stitched into the center opening.

★ Make buds with 2 petals.

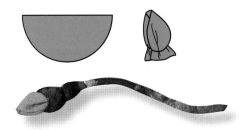

★ Use an assortment of green fabrics for the leaves.

Note: The bluebird in the wreath is not the state bird, which is the western meadowlark. I used artistic license and just added it for its grace and beauty.

OHIO

17th state—March 1, 1803

23" × 23"
Made and machine quilted by the author
(Pattern and flower, state, and historical information on the CD)

Scarlet Carnation—fond memories, ancient roots

Design Area	10" square
Block Size	14" square
Wreath Type	Simple circle
Techniques	Appliqué, silk ribbon work, Ultrasuede appliqué, floss embroidery
Design Source	Traditional

Flower Construction

This wreath is made of appliquéd fabric for the wreath (stem), Ultrasuede leaves, and silk ribbon dimensional flowers. This technique works well with 1 yard of soft Hanah 1" or 1½" wide bias silk for each carnation using 8 yards total.

★ Ruffle or distress the outer edge by pulling the ribbon against one blade of a pair of scissors. You can also run your thumb nail against the ribbon and produce a slightly frayed but ruffled edge. It is faster with the scissors.

★ Stitch the entire length of the ribbon close to the selvage edge and gather tightly.

★ Roll the gathered ribbon to form the flower and stitch the raw end under at the end.

(Continued on page 57)

OHIO

★ To form the green stem bases of the carnation, take 6" of 1" wide green ribbon either wired or un-wired and wrap around stitched gathers on the raw-edge end of the flower.

★ Stitch the green ribbon to the bottom edge as you wrap. Go around twice forming a tightly coiled base.

★ Do not cut the ribbon. Squeeze the base of the green coil and stitch through the base to form a narrow end.

★ Twirl the remaining length of ribbon to form a twisted stem. *Note: If using unwired ribbon, this may not work.*

★ Leaves are Ultrasuede appli-qué with green outline accent embroidery on the outside edges.

OKLAHOMA

Incorporated as the 46th state on November 16, 1907

21" × 21"
Made and hand and machine quilted by the author
(Pattern and flower, state, and historical information on the CD)

Mistletoe—endearing and poisonous

Design Area	7" square
Block Size	12" square
Wreath Type	Inverted crossed branches
Techniques	Floss embroidery, beadwork
Design Source	Traditional album design

Flower Construction

Edge quilting with embroidery echoes the central design of this quilt.

★ Embroider the main stem with several layers of outline stitch.

★ Use a template to trace the leaves and fill in with the outline stitch using 2 different shades of green floss for contrast.

★ Use 4mm round ivory beads for the berries for a realistic effect. If you can't find the right color beads, then use large French knots instead.

OREGON

33rd state—February 14, 1859

19" × 19"
Made and hand quilted by the author
(Pattern and flower, state, and historical information on the CD)

Oregon Grape—neither holly nor grape, it's better food for birds than people

Design Area	7½" × 8½"
Block Size	12" square
Wreath Type	Traditional crossed branches
Techniques	Silk ribbon embroidery, appliqué
Design Source	Traditional album design

Flower Construction

This quilt has a crossed branch design with strong quilting echoes that add dimension.

Embroider the main stem, side stems, flowers, and berries on appliquéd leaves.

★ Embroider the main stem with pearl cotton.

★ Appliqué the leaves. Embroider an outline and center vein.

★ Use Superior Threads variegated silk ribbon for the flowers and berries:

★ **Flowers:** one 5-yard package of 2mm #100 Sunflower.

★ Make the French knots for the flowers with 3 twists.

★ **Berries:** two 3-yard packages of 7mm #132 Blue Iris.

★ Make the French knots for the berries with 3 twists.

PENNSYLVANIA
2nd state*—December 17, 1787
*One of four commonwealths in the nation

26" x 26"
Made by the author and machine quilted by Ellen Peters
(Pattern and flower, state, and historical information on the CD)

Mountain Laurel—evergreen, showy, and poisonous

Design Area	13" x 12"
Block Size	13" square
Wreath Type	Closed circle
Techniques	Appliqué, ribbon work
Design Source	Original interpretation of a closed circular wreath

Flower Construction

Make 2 clusters of 7 flowerettes and 2 clusters with 3 flowerettes each. You'll need 2 yards of ribbon; each mountain laurel flowerette requires 3" of #3 (½" wide) wired pink/white ombré ribbon.

★ Cut ribbon into 3" lengths. Remove the wire from the edge that will become the center of the flower. Centers may be pink or white or a mixture of both.

★ Fold the ribbon in half lengthwise and sew the raw edges together with a ⅛" seam.

★ Turn this "tube" inside out. Use a double thread and stitch a row of running stitches ¼" down from the unwired or center edge.

(Continued on page 61)

PENNSYLVANIA

★ Pull and gather tightly. Secure with a backstitch/knot. Spread the flowerettes open to lie fairly flat.

★ Add a gold bead in the center. Mold the outer wired edge up and toward the center to form a cup-like flowerette.

★ Continue making flowerettes and cluster them in groups. Arrange and attach on a piece of crinoline.

★ Secure the final arrangements to the wreath and background fabric with several hidden stitches.

RHODE ISLAND
13th state—May 29, 1790

22" x 22"
Made and hand quilted by the author
(Pattern and flower, state, and historical information on the CD)

Violet—weed to some, flower to most

Design Area	10" square
Block Size	13½" square
Wreath Type	Closed circle
Techniques	Appliqué, couching, ribbon work
Design Source	Original

Flower Construction

The branches are made with 3 different couched trims. The leaves are appliquéd and the flowers are ruched wire-edged ribbon. Make 10–12 violets and arrange them in a pleasing manner on the base of heart-shaped violet leaves. This is the simplest ruched flower to make as you only need to stitch 3 triangles to form a flower.

★ Use 1½ yards of #9 (1½" wide) ombré purple wired ribbon. Cut 4½" of ribbon per flower. Unwired ribbon may be used but the petal shape is harder to control.

★ Fold the ribbon in half and pinch the wire edges to form creases in the wire. Fold the ribbon in half again and repeat the pinching.

★ Unfold the ribbon and place pins in the pinched creases. These serve as your stitching guides.

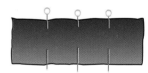

(Continued on page 63)

RHODE ISLAND

★ Stitch a ruching pattern, taking care to loop the thread over the top and bottom of the selvage edge when changing stitching directions. Gently gather as tightly as possible and secure with backstitches.

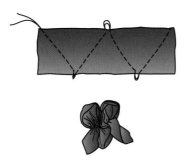

Note: If you are using bias silk ribbon, your violet is complete at this step. Simply add a bead or two to the center.

★ With wire-edged ribbon, trim off the tails to about ¼". Be careful not to trim too close to the stitched petals or you'll have trouble with the next step.

★ Tuck the tails beneath and secure with a few stitches. Pick up a bead while taking these stitches and you accomplish two jobs with one stitch.

★ For each bud, cut a 1½" square of ribbon. Remove the wire from both sides and stitch all around the edges. Gather to form a yo-yo and flatten it to form a gathered bud. Turn the raw edges under and embroider a green bud cap at the top edge to attach to the stem. Embroider stems for the buds using the outline stitch.

Helpful hints for stems:

★ Use silk cording and 2 different trims in the wreath, each in a different shade and texture, to add interest.

★ Draw intertwining stem lines on the background fabric using a light box. Use a toothpick to place dots of white glue on the stem lines. Glue-baste the cording and trims to hold them in place until you couch them down.

South Carolina

8th state—May 23, 1788

24" x 24"
Made and hand and machine quilted by the author
(Pattern and flower, state, and historical information on the CD)

Yellow Jessamine—like many a Southern belle, beautiful and bad

Design Area	10" x 11"
Block Size	14" x 13"
Wreath Type	L-shaped, asymmetrical, branching, naturalistic design
Techniques	Appliqué, floss embroidery
Design Source	Inspired by an antique block

Flower Construction

The wreath is made from appliquéd blossoms, buds, and leaves with embroidered tendrils twining around the main stem and branches. The flowers are outlined with embroidery floss.

★ Draw the templates for the flowers and buds.

★ Appliqué the flowers in place. Don't worry about exact placement; just position as you like for a pleasing arrangement.

★ Add beads to the flower centers.

★ Embroider the twining vine with 2 strands of floss.

★ Attach the buds to the tiny stems with 3 lazy daisy stitches.

★ Do the background quilting in gold metallic thread in a sunburst design against the blue sky fabric to give an added dimension to the wreath.

SOUTH DAKOTA

40th state—November 2, 1889

16" x 16"
Made and hand and machine quilted by the author
(Pattern and flower, state, and historical information on the CD)

Pasque Flower—the ever-growing Easter bloom

Design Area	7½" square
Block Size	10" square
Wreath Type	Star-shaped with intersecting stems
Techniques	Fabrico markers, floss embroidery
Design Source	Original

Flower Construction

These flowers are really fun to make using Fabrico markers. Enjoy a pleasant experience from your childhood days of coloring in the lines. The twisted stems are embroidered.

★ Draw the flowers on the background fabric with a pencil and a light touch.

★ Outline with dark purple Fabrico color #116 Peony and shade with light purple #136 Wisteria, leaving the center area white or uncolored.

★ Add darker streaks of purple for shading.

★ Add yellow in the center and accent with French knots.

★ Draw the buds with a black Pigma pen outline, then shade in with colors #116 Peony and #136 Wisteria.

TENNESSEE
16th state—June 1, 1796

23" × 23"
Made by the author and machine quilted by Ellen Peters
(Pattern and flower, state, and historical information on the CD)

Iris—wild, yet tame and beautiful

Design Area	11" square
Block Size	14" square
Wreath Type	Square paper-cut wreath
Techniques	Appliqué, floss embroidery
Design Source	Vintage album pattern from an antique Baltimore album, quiltmaker unknown

Flower Construction

Appliquéd petals with embroidered stems using the outline stitch and sashiko stitch "shadow" leaves create this square wreath.

★ Appliqué the flowers using fussy-cut petal sections from shaded fabric.

★ Stitch shadow leaves using the sashiko stitch.

★ Use doubled embroidery floss to stitch the stems.

★ Embroider French knots for the flower centers using yellow floss.

TEXAS
28th state—December 29, 1845

27" x 27"
Made and machine quilted by the author
(Pattern and flower, state, and historical information on the CD)

Bluebonnet—beauty gracing uncultivated places

Design Area	12½" square
Block Size	16" square
Wreath Type	Large pieced star
Techniques	Piecing, ribbon work
Design Source	Traditional pieced block, the Texas Star circa 1867, from *The Romance of the Patchwork Quilt in America* by Carrie A. Hall and Rose G. Kretsinger, 1935

Flower Construction

The center star is made of a variety of golden fabrics. The radiating points are sky blue, green, and bluebonnet print peaks. The sky blue points are accented with dimensional ribbon bluebonnets. The flowers are stitched separately onto crinoline, then appliquéd in place on the rays. The Texas state flower fabric was used in the star and for the border. This is great fabric if you can still find it.

★ Piece the Star block.

★ For the bluebonnets use 1 yard of #3 (¾" wide) ombré blue ribbon per flower, 8 yards total.

★ Trace the bluebonnet shape on crinoline.

(Continued on page 68)

TEXAS

★ Stitch down the middle of the ribbon and gather ribbon to about 10" in length, then arrange on crinoline.

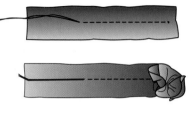

★ Position the ribbon on the crinoline so that no white of the background shows. You can squeeze the ribbon into the shape you desire. That's the beauty of working with wire-edged ribbon. Stitch the ribbon between the folds to hold it in place.

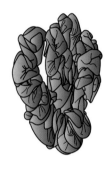

★ Trim away excess crinoline.

★ Position on the star's rays and sew in place. I used fabric glue instead of sewing for a flat, smooth look.

Utah
45th state—January 4, 1896

SEGO LILY
Calochortus nuttallii

16" x 16"
Made and hand and machine quilted by the author
(Pattern and flower, state, and historical information on the CD)

Sego Lily—plant and animal mimicry, animal and human nutrition

Design Area	9" square
Block Size	10" square
Wreath Type	Simple wreath
Technique	Drawn and colored blossoms
Design Source	Original

Flower Construction

Custom color each petal with Fabrico markers for a realistic effect.

★ Trace the flower petals with a template and cut out.

★ Accent the center tips of the petals with drawn and colored-in details using #156 Brick Red, #111 Lemon Yellow, and #112 Tangerine.

★ Draw a 5½" diameter circle in the center of the background fabric as a placement guide for the flowers.

★ Appliqué the flower petals in place and form a circle, leaving space in between each of the flowers.

★ Embroider leaves and buds between the flowers to add greenery and accent the wreath design. Use outline and fill-in stitches.

★ Use a stencil for the lettering. Draw the outline, then color in with markers. Outline embroider using 2 strands of variegated King Tut quilting thread as the final accent to make the lettering stand out.

VERMONT

14th state—March 4, 1791

22" × 22"
Made by the author and machine quilted by Ellen Peters
(Pattern and flower, state, and historical information on the CD)

Red Clover—sweet source of fertility and good health

Design Area	11" square
Block Size	14½" square
Wreath Type	Partially opened entwined circle
Techniques	Appliqué, Ultrasuede appliqué, floss embroidery, stump work
Design Source	Original

Flower Construction

Appliquéd stems are entwined with Ultrasuede leaves and embroidered, stump work clover blossoms.

★ **Stems:** Appliqué ¼" bias binding in place. Use 2 different brown fabrics for contrast—striped and solid. Overlap the strips for a twisted effect.

★ **Leaves:** Cut leaves from Ultrasuede. Stitch in place using matching thread. Use a single strand of embroidery floss for a finishing outline stitch along the outer edges of the leaves.

★ **Blossoms:** Use a variegated, dark, pinkish-red color of sashiko cotton thread or 3 strands of embroidery floss for the blossoms.

★ Cut 4 felt circles ⅞", ¾", ⅝", and ½" for each of the blossoms. The color of the felt should be neutral or close to the pink color of your thread.

★ Stack the circles like a wedding cake and stitch together through the centers.

(Continued on page 71)

VERMONT

★ Invert the "cake" so the smallest tier is on the bottom against the background fabric.

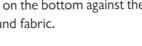

★ Cut a larger circle of plain fabric (a generous ¼" larger than the largest circle). Stitch around the edges and gather over the felt for a fabric-covered surface for embroidery.

Optional: add a four-leaf clover to your wreath.

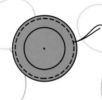

★ Embroider over the felt or fabric surface using irregular length staggered stitches to completely cover the surface.

★ Use longer, staggered stitches at the base and fill in with shorter stitches.

VIRGINIA
10th state*—June 25, 1788
*One of four commonwealths in the nation

20" × 20"
Made and hand quilted by the author
(Pattern and flower, state and historical information on the CD)

Dogwood—gentle tree acting as flower

Design Area	11½" square
Block Size	13" square
Wreath Type	Closed circle
Techniques	Appliqué, ribbon work
Design Source	Original

Flower Construction

Both appliquéd fabric and ribbon form the flowers in this wreath.

★ Use chintz for the appliqué fabric and seed beads for the flower centers. Make 4 fabric flowers.

★ You'll need 17" of #5 (1" wide) pink/white ombré ribbon for each ribbon flower (1½ yards total). Make 3 flowers and a bud. Use the square U technique—4" per petal.

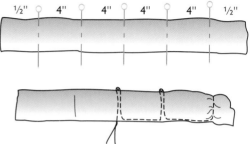

★ Use knotted trim for the flower centers.

★ After the petals are gathered, anchor them onto crinoline to form a circle.

★ Sculpt or mold the petals by elongating each petal slightly, separating them from the other petals and turn the outer center edges under.

★ Dimple or pinch the top center of each petal to form the dogwood's notch and anchor this notch to the crinoline with a hidden stitch.

★ Trim away the excess crinoline and position the flowers on the wreath; anchor in place.

★ Use assorted green prints and shades for the appliquéd leaves.

★ To make the bow, use vintage French ombré blue ribbon, tie it in a bow, and appliqué it in place. This is the easiest way to appliqué a bow and make it look real.

WASHINGTON
42nd state—November 11, 1889

16" x 14"
Made and hand quilted by the author
(Pattern and flower, state, and historical information on the CD)

Coast Rhododendron—toxic but quick to grow

Design Area	13" x 7"
Block Size	16" x 14"
Wreath Type	Postcard format of a landscape with a floral base
Techniques	Appliqué, silk ribbon embroidery, Fabrico marker, floss embroidery
Design Source	Original

Flower Construction

Skydyes hand-painted fabrics provided the perfect background, mountain, and foliage.

★ Trace the shape of Mt. Rainier and appliqué it onto the background fabric.

★ Draw 3 circles on a separate piece of light purple fabric for the bases for the floral embroidery—one 3½" diameter center circle and two 2½" diameter circles. Draw the circles about 1" apart from each other.

★ Using a pencil, draw a series of guide circles inside the larger circles, using a light touch. Have the smaller circles overlap each other. Draw a center point inside each circle to help center the petals. The flower petals will be embroidered inside these guide circles.

Note: These guide circles are optional if you wish to just go for it!

★ Embroider the blossoms using Superior Threads variegated silk ribbon 7mm #112 Hydrangea or #111 Berry. You will need 2 packages of 3 yards each.

(Continued on page 74)

WASHINGTON

★ Make 5 or 6 petals for each flower with the curled leaf stitch within the smaller circles.

★ When the circles are filled with flowers, trim away the excess fabric leaving a ½" margin. Turn this edge under and appliqué the flowers onto the postcard fabric. Attach a few more final petals onto the background fabric to hide the edge of the purple fabric.

★ Stitch a bead in the center of each flower.

Note: Some flowers may have just a few petals to fill in spaces.

★ Use a stencil to trace the letters of the state name onto the postcard. Use Fabrico markers to color in the letters.

★ Embroider the outline of each letter with a single strand of silver metallic thread. Use this thread for hand or machine quilting the clouds and leaves.

WEST VIRGINIA
35th state—June 20, 1863

BIG LAUREL
Rhododendrom maximum

22" x 20"
Made by the author and machine quilted by Ellen Peters
(Pattern and flower, state, and historical information on the CD)

Big Laurel—big, bold, and beautiful

Design Area	10" square
Block Size	13" x 12"
Wreath Type	Open laurel victory wreath
Techniques	Appliqué, ribbon work
Design Source	Original

Flower Construction

You will need 2 yards of #9 (1½" wide) light pink wire-edged ribbon. Use a soft pink that combines two different textures to make a beautiful blossom.

★ Ruche a zigzag pattern of triangles at 3" intervals. Be sure that the thread loops over the top and bottom edges of the ribbon before stitching the diagonal sides of the triangles.

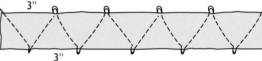

★ Pull the thread and gently gather after stitching 2 or 3 triangles. Gather the ribbon to a length of 15".

★ Spread the petals open so they are rounded in shape. Fold the bottom petals up so they lie between the top petals. Do this for about 6".

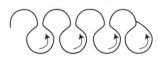

★ Draw a 3" diameter circle on a square of crinoline.

★ Arrange the ribbon petals in a tight center circle on a crinoline base and secure from behind with a pin to hold it in place.

(Continued on page 76)

WEST VIRGINIA

★ Tuck the second row behind the center, taking care to keep the petals all going upward. Arrange a third row if necessary.

★ Anchor the petals in place using hidden stitches.

★ Sew beads in a scattered manner over the flower's petals.

★ Trim away the excess crinoline and secure onto your background fabric.

★ Embroider at the seam edge between the border and block background fabric using 3 strands of floss for an easy effect similar to piping.

★ Embroider all around the leaves for contrast.

WISCONSIN

30th state—May 29, 1848

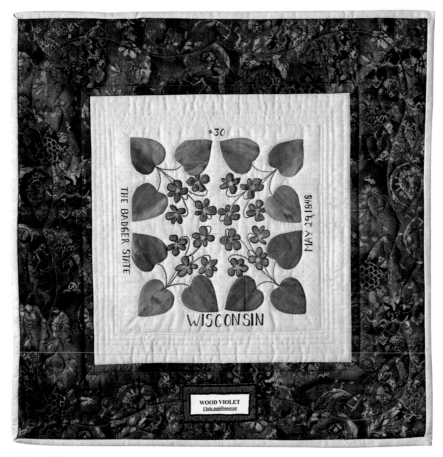

21" x 21"
Made and hand quilted by the author and machine quilted by Ellen Peters
(Pattern and flower, state, and historical information on the CD)

Wood Violet—such a pretty weed

Design Area	9" square
Block Size	13" square
Wreath Type	Square wreath
Techniques	Appliqué, Fabrico marker
Design Source	From *Garden View Appliqué* by Faye Labanaris (AQS, 2002)

Flower Construction

Leaves are appliquéd using Skydyes fabric. The flowers are painted or colored in using Pam Holland's drappliqué technique.

★ Appliqué the heart-shaped fabric leaves in place.

★ Trace the shape of the violet flower onto the background fabric using a template and a light touch with a lead mechanical pencil.

★ Outline with black marker leaving the center area open for the yellow coloring to be added last.

★ Use Fabrico markers to color in the violets, first with #136 Wisteria. Let them dry before proceeding to the next step. Use a streaking motion or pattern instead of fill-in coloring. Be sure to leave some white spaces in the background fabric.

★ Streak or shade the petals with #116 Peony from the center on out. Let dry before proceeding to the next step.

★ Color in the center area with #111 Lemon Yellow. Draw the stems in green with black shading.

WYOMING
44th state—July 10, 1890

24" x 24"
Made and hand and machine quilted by the author
(Pattern and flower, state, and historical information on the CD)

Indian Paintbrush—dangerous beauty

Design Area   7" square
Block Size   13" square
Wreath Type   A bouquet of flower stems tied with a ribbon
Technique   Fabrico markers
Design Source   Original

Flower Construction

These flowers are sketched onto the background fabric, then colored in with Fabrico markers. The state flower fabric for Wyoming was used for the border fabric.

★ Sketch the bracts of the plant onto the background fabric first with a hard lead pencil, then outline with a fine point marker. Practice first on paper so you get your design technique down pat.

★ Shade the bracts first with #114 Poppy Red in the lower portion, then use #112 Tangerine in the upper portion. Finally, streak the petals with #156 Brick for a shaded effect.

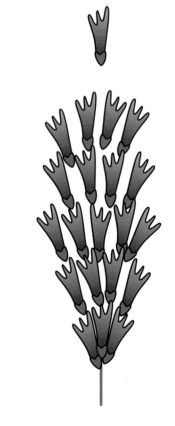

★ Add #121 Emerald Green to the base of the bract. Be sure to leave white space between the bracts.

★ Draw the ribbon as a flowing tie and outline with fine point black marker.

About the Author

Faye Labanaris specializes in hand appliqué, including Baltimore Album and Hawaiian styles, and in dimensional ribbonwork appliqué and embroidery made with wire-edged and silk ribbons.

Faye enjoys teaching and eagerly shares her knowledge with her students. She offers classes to all levels of quilters, inspiring beginners as well as challenging advanced quilters. She has taught in Hawaii and throughout the continental United States and Great Britain. She has written five books: *Blossoms by the Sea—Making Ribbon Flowers for Quilts*; *Quilts with a View—A Fabric Adventure*; *Garden View Appliqué—Vintage Album Patterns*; *Appliqué Rose Garden*; and *Ribbon Treasures from Celia's Garden*, all published by the American Quilter's Society.

In 1994, she was voted National Honored Teacher by her students in the first C&T Publishing and Elly Sienkiewicz Baltimore Album Revival Contest. Her quilt, A TRIBUTE TO CELIA THAXTER, placed first in its category, Reflective of a Particular Life and Time, and was also considered for *The Twentieth Century's Best American Quilts, Celebrating 100 Years of Quiltmaking*. That quilt became the basis for her first book, *Blossoms by the Sea*. Her quilt, AN ENGLISH COTTAGE GARDEN, placed third in the Innovative category in the second Baltimore Revival contest. That quilt inspired Faye to write *Garden View Appliqué*.

Faye is the co-producer and founder of Quilt Hawaii, a quilt show and conference held each year in early July on a different Hawaiian island. She also co-produces Quilt Ventures Tours for Quilters with tours throughout the Northeast. She lives in Dover, New Hampshire, with her husband, Nick. He and their two sons have been very supportive of her endeavors.

Visit **www.quiltventures.com** for more information about Quilt Hawaii and Quilt Ventures Tours.

more AQS Books

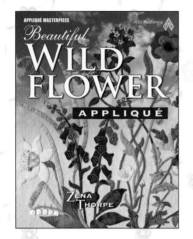 T his is only a small selection of the books available from the American Quilter's Society. AQS books are known worldwide for timely topics, clear writing, beautiful color photos, and accurate illustrations and patterns. The following books are available from your local bookseller, quilt shop, or public library.

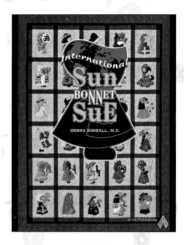

#8526

#8355

#8347

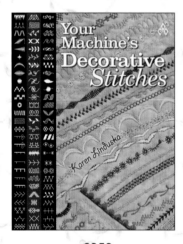

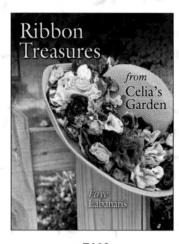

#8353

#7610

#8351

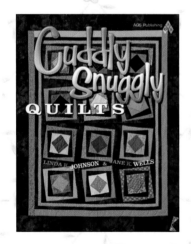

#8239

#7484

#8242

LOOK for these books nationally.
CALL or **VISIT** our website at

1-800-626-5420
www.AmericanQuilter.com